The Gospel of

JOSEPH OF ARIMATHEA

Also by James Harpur

Poetry:

The Dark Age (Anvil Press, 2007)
Oracle Bones (Anvil Press, 2001)
The Monk's Dream (Anvil Press, 1996)
A Vision of Comets (Anvil Press, 1993)

Translation:

Fortune's Prisoner: The Poems of Boethius's Consolation of Philosophy

Non-fiction:

Love Burning in the Soul: The Story of the Christian Mystics, from Saint Paul to Thomas Merton (Shambhala, 2005)

The Gospel of

JOSEPH OF ARIMATHEA

James Harpur

WILD GOOSE PUBLICATIONS

© James Harpur

First published 2007 by
Wild Goose Publications
4th Floor, Savoy House, 140 Sauchiehall St, Glasgow G2 3DH, UK.
Wild Goose Publications is the publishing division of the Iona Community.
Scottish Charity No. SCO03794. Limited Company Reg. No. SCO96243.
www.ionabooks.com

ISBN 978-1-905010-35-6

The publishers gratefully acknowledge the support of the Drummond Trust,
3 Pitt Terrace, Stirling FK8 2EY in producing this book.

The author was supported in the writing of this book by Cork Arts Council

A catalogue record for this book is available from the British Library.

Overseas distribution:
Australia: Willow Connection Pty Ltd, Unit 4A, 3-9 Kenneth Road,
Manly Vale, NSW 2093
New Zealand: Pleroma, Higginson Street, Otane 4170, Central Hawkes Bay
N. America: Novalis/Bayard, 10 Lower Spadina Ave., Suite 400, Toronto,
Ontario M5V 2Z

Printed by Cromwell Press, Trowbridge, Wiltshire

In memory of J. Krishnamurti (1895–1986)

Acknowledgements

Poems in this collection have previously been published in the following periodicals: *Agenda, Scintilla, Southword.*

The poem 'Joseph' was a runner-up in the *Scintilla* Long Poem competition, 2004.

A number of people helped me in the making of this book and I'm very grateful for their encouragement and insights. I'd like to thank Anna Adams, Mary O'Connell, Elizabeth Rapp, Evie and Grace, and Pat and Mel; and in particular for their detailed comments: Rosemary Canavan, Alyson Hallett, Christopher Southgate, James Turner and Ian Wild. I would also like to say thanks to my old Divinity teachers at school, Willie Booth and Alan Megahey, who set me on my way. And Sandra and Neil of Wild Goose, for guiding this book smoothly into port.

Some of this book was conceived during a poetry residency at Exeter Cathedral in 2001, and I would like to thank the Dean and Chapter for their warm hospitality. Many thanks, too, to Ian McDonagh and Cork Arts for a generous bursary that helped me to finish the book.

CONTENTS

'Now there was a man named Joseph, a member of the Council, a good and upright man ... He came from the Judean town of Arimathea and he was waiting on the kingdom of God. Going to Pilate, he asked for Jesus' body.'

Luke: 23:50

'And did those feet in ancient time ...'

William Blake, Preface to Milton: a Poem

'A fourth method consists in the use of simple imagination, when we represent to ourselves the Saviour in his sacred humanity as if he were near us, just as we sometimes imagine a friend to be present, and say, "I imagine that I see such a one who is doing this or that," or "I seem to see him" or something similar.'

St Francis de Sales, from The Introduction to the Devout Life

Prologue

This is how it stood between myself and Jesus of Nazareth. My eldest brother married the sister of his mother, Mary, and I was like an older cousin to him. After he was executed stories circulated. Some said he was a prophet, even 'the anointed one'. Some thought he was a healer and a preacher; a few believed he was a revolutionary who would have brought forward the great rebellion by forty years, if he had survived.

Our lives were set on different paths and intersected rarely, until the end. Of course I heard about him from afar, from time to time, and I recall him as a youth. Once when I was a much younger man I had to travel to the west, beyond the Pillars of Hercules – I was a merchant dealing in the luxury market – and I took the young Jesus with me to let him taste the world beyond Judea. The journey still burns brightly in my memory. He was quiet on the outward voyage, no doubt disorientated by his first time on the sea. And it was cold and wet and grey as soon as we passed the Pillars.

We were heading for the island of the tin mines, where our Roman masters had established a number of trading posts. Our ship came to rest in a small place known as Oppidum Maris. It lies beside the estuary of a river, the boundary between two tribes, and cliffs that roll along in dullish sanguine. Nearby, the local people gather salt, quarry stone and tan hides.

Here at last, back on dry land – although it remained cold and damp despite being springtime – the lad became his usual self, engaging and alert. He was amazed by the great piles of hides laid out on the shingle, the gangs of shivering, pale-skinned slaves, dogs the size of ponies, and pretty ornaments in copper and gold. He sat in on the barterings I had with local dealers, rough-looking men, long-

haired, red-faced, but with a certain nobility in their long cloaks –
and with a great desire for wine and, my speciality, spices. I remember him laughing at my enthusiastic attempts at sign language and
pidgin Latin.

We stayed for several days. One afternoon we walked inland to
stretch our legs and see something of the country. Turning west we
trekked along a river the locals called the 'Culli', picking our way
through woods that bordered it on either bank. Late spring, and
blue flowers were flowing through small ponds of sunlight. We did
not talk, but I could see he was amazed by the blaze of colours, the
density of trees, a clearing with the greenest grass he'd ever seen.
'Like Indian emeralds,' he said, remembering those I had once
shown him.

At length, about two miles from where we'd turned off westward,
we climbed a hill that lay to the north; and near the crossing of two
drovers' paths we found a pool fed by a spring, sheltered from behind
by a gouge in the hill. We sat and drank, then gazed across the glowing valley – it looked as if it had just been created by the hand of
God. A line of paler green marked out the trees beside the river. A
few yards to our left, three yellow butterflies were intertwining in a
dance above a larger stone. 'This must be paradise,' I recall him
saying with a sigh, 'the sort of place you'd wish to be for eternity.'
And I agreed with him. Then we fell into an enchanted silence.

The voyage home was uneventful. We had been invigorated by
our trip, by all the strangeness, the refreshing climate, and I at least
was dreading going back to our desperate country, the hardened
faces of the occupying forces, the hardened faces of the zealots. It
was as if the river of God's love had evaporated and left a stream of
dry and dusty jagged rocks.

Towards the last months of his life, a number of people came to me with questions: 'You know him, you are family – what's the truth about him? What is he like? Is he the one?' All I could reply was that I had known him for a short while, many years ago. To tell the truth, I was sceptical of what he had become, or what they said he had become ... until, one time, I heard him speaking in the Temple. He was inspired. I'd never heard such passion, such conviction; it was as if the words had become living things, like tiny creatures of light, and we were absorbing them. If God speaks through human beings, He was doing so then. Soon after that they killed him.

I did my best for him at the end. I hope he would have approved, but there was little time to react – his execution came so suddenly, despite the warning signs. What I carried out was relatively easy to accomplish, and I wanted to help him find peace, and help the movement he had started. For many years I have thought about my action and wondered. 'Seeds grow in mystery,' a rabbi once said to me. I did it for myself as much as for his followers. It was at this time that I received a dream or vision – something I'm not prone to – in which he spoke to me. I took it as his blessing and shall remember it until the day I die.

The vision altered my life: for the first time I had a sense of profound purpose. It set in motion my quest to find out for myself who Jesus really was, by seeking out and questioning those who knew him in a way I never did – his closest friends, family and followers. A few I knew quite well, and one or two I'd met briefly, and there were others I'd never met before. Some of these witnesses I came across just after he was put to death, and some I sought in later years.

At first I thought of writing nothing down. I simply listened to their tales of meeting Jesus. On leaving them I would recall each story and try to shape it in a way I would remember. Eventually, wishing to preserve these recollections, I wrote them down in Aramaic. Then after pestering by some Gentile friends, and with the onset of old age, I translated them, with some assistance, into Greek. Before each recollection I added a few notes to remind myself how and when I had met each witness. The order of the stories more or less followed the sequence of Jesus's life and final days. I added at the end my own story, including the vision that sparked the quest.

The people I interviewed were drawing on memories that had been modified by time. Their words became in turn part of my own memory, with its legion of personal biases and impressions. Finally, when I was writing down the stories I had to find words in one language, then translate them into another. What truth survives a process such as this! What are our lives but a constant shifting from one dimension to another, from the mental to the material and back again, always circling truth but never getting nearer, like an ox around a millstone? And yet how else can we investigate the mysteries of the truth?

I recorded these memories to find out who Jesus was. Whether I have found his spirit, or mine, or that of others, I do not really know. In any case I place this scroll within this jar, which I will hide within a certain cave, and pray to God that if it is discovered in the future, it may reveal its secrets and rescue from the darkness a man who made a difference to so many lives.

NATHANAEL

1

One day I came to Cana, set among vineyards and olive groves several miles northeast of Nazareth. It was there Jesus had once gone to a wedding – his attendance had become the stuff of local legend. Apparently he had the knack of changing atmospheres without really saying or doing much. With a frown or laugh, word or gesture, he could invigorate proceedings, or calm them down. If he was melancholic, he could affect those close to him for days.

In Cana I made enquiries about a man named Nathanael, someone who, people told me, had an interesting story to tell. I gathered that he had been a rather spiky, cynical individual. In due course I tracked him down, and we sat outside beneath his grand old fig tree, watching as the ridge of hills beyond grew shadowy. I was surprised to find him relaxed and happy with his lot. His children sat with us, watching me with silent interest. Then jumping to their feet, as if possessed by spirits of decisiveness, they climbed the tree and giggled in the branches, from which they hung and dropped, got up and climbed the tree again in a cycle of merriment.

Nathanael

So this is how it happened.
I was sitting by this very tree
As usual gazing at the sky
Through a frame of dipping leaves
And seeing nothing.
As usual my soul was numb;
The thought of doing anything
Disintegrated in futility.

I stared at fields migrating
Beneath the sudden light and dark of clouds
Towards the visible horizon,
Beyond which more horizons stretched
Into anywhere; my heart had shrunk,
Cut off from love, will, anything.

I sat and sat, trapped
Inside the dead routines of mind
Inside the tyranny of family
Inside a gently dying body
The centre of a lengthening line
Of countless unknown ancestors
Rotted inside their cells of earth,
And unborn progeny
Waiting to join the pointlessness,
The pointless endlessness of life.

And then the miracle began.
I remember Philip out of breath,
Spittle from his mouth –
He'd met him – 'Who?' – 'the holy one!'
He tugged at me to come. Curious
To see the face behind the fuss
I walked behind him on the track
That led through fields and vineyards past
The huddled leprous shacks around
The outskirts of the town, until
We finally reached the marketplace.

He was scratching something in the dust,

Teaching, I guessed, the alphabet
To peasants squatting by his feet.
He stopped, stood up as I drew near.
He looked too slight, too hollow-cheeked,
A cliché of the wandering prophet.
My heart was hardening in my glare.
He said he came from Nazareth.
'A prophet from Nazareth, no less!' –
My tone was smirky, I admit.
He looked at me and thought a while
Then closed his eyes, and opened them.
'A drinker of self-pity, no less,'
He paused (I'm sure I saw a smile)
'Beneath an undeserving fig tree.'
I watched him watching my confusion
Then felt a softness, a blossoming,
A wave of warmth break over me
Dislodging something from myself –
Again I blurted something odd,
It was embarrassingly glib:
'It's true – you are the son of God!'
At that he winced theatrically
And shot a finger to his lip.

Later, we took a stroll alone
Beside a vineyard on a slope
A mile or so beyond the town;
Grapes were fattening on the vines.
The evening sun drew out my thoughts;
I talked about my dead-end life,

The claustrophobia of the past,
The frightening spaces of the future.
And all he did was listen,
Gazing ahead or at his feet.
I talked until my mouth was dry,
My soul was empty.

We walked in silence. Then he spoke:
'Captivity, Nathanael,
Arises from the heart and mind,
Which draw their dragnets through the waters
Of memory and trap the things
That reassure and feel benign –
Cana with its homely tatty streets
The flowing hills of Galilee
The faces of your wife and children –
The more you try to keep a thing
Beyond the instant that it's there,
There, full of life, the more it rots
And traps you in its ripe decay.
Forget the bad, forget the good,
Throw back the memories you've caught
And let your spirit rove across
The world without accumulating –
Like a wind that passes through a tree
But does not bear away its leaves –
Then you may enter Jacob's vision
No matter where you are on earth –
At home or in a foreign land
In open fields or in a prison ...'

Just then I seemed to lose his voice
Or heard it as a murmuring
And felt an inner benediction –
As if I were complete, contained,
Desiring nothing for myself
And all my fears had turned to joy;
I stopped, and fell away, drifted
Into a zone of silence, wonder:
Beyond, as in a far-off land
Yet clearly visible, I saw
A stair of light materialise,
A stair that rose up to the sky
And angels moving up and down,
Gliding between the earth and heaven
Delightfully and endlessly –
And then I heard his words again,
'Their ladder is the path of love
And if you find it you will see
That everywhere belongs to you,
For home becomes the place you are
And there can be no boundary
No east or west, below, above.'

AZOR

2

Many people remembered the time he healed a man beside Bethesda pool in Jerusalem. I myself had heard about it in the streets and markets soon after it occurred. So once when visiting the city I sought this person out. Of course I knew Jesus's reputation as a healer, but I wanted to know first-hand how it felt to have your body restored. The man's name, I was told, was Azor.

Directed to the south of town, I called into dark interiors in endless narrow streets. Eventually my 'Azor of Bethesda' met a croaked response. He slowly greeted me, nudging forward, with one hand perched upon a stick like the bony beak of some great bird. Hearing my request he nodded, led me in. At very little prompting he spoke, and as he mined his memory his face grew bright. He'd gone to live in Bethesda after his father had died, and there was no one left to care for him. He'd been unable to walk since early childhood. At first the pool had been a shock: the monotony, watching the shadows slink round all day long, the stink of urine. But there were constant visitors, and more charity than at home. There was always, too, the prospect of the visit of the healing angel.

Azor

I saw the angel only once.
One ordinary morning
The imprecations, moaning, chants,
Drifting from the shady portico
Around the pool, began to falter –
I was alert, unsure if I alone
Could hear the silence fall like dust
And feel another world opening;

And then the light began to alter –
Just as at dawn the silhouettes
Of woods, a tree or hill
Assume a tincture of violet
And the solemn earth begins to rise
Gradation by gradation till
The sun, a rim of runny orange,
Flashes, attracts the eye –
So the colours were intensified,
The water threaded with gold lines
The columns glowing deepest ivory.

Then by the pool a shapeless light
Became the contours of a man
With wings, a pastel rainbow round him
Except above his head, where blue
As pure as sky was hovering.
Suddenly out of nowhere
A breeze whipped up, brisk, cold,
Freshening the stagnant atmosphere.
The angel gestured at the water –
All this was still in silence –
And rapt, unable but to stare,
I caught a movement in the shadows:
Someone was shuffling – out he came
Bent double, inching to the edge,
Squinting at the glare, poised
To break the surface of the pool.
He plunged, sprang up and down and up –
Droplets tumbling from his hair,

Glistening as from sacred oil –
His face was sleek with radiance
His hands were cupping up the water.

He left the pool to close itself.
The atmosphere grew less intense
The angel's form began to fade
And coughing, groans returned, a swarm
Of mumbled prayers of gratitude,
A psalm of David touched the air.

My time came shortly afterwards.
Another day devoid of grace,
Of watching shadows slide around.
I heard my name, as in a whisper,
Or in a wind or distant rush of waves,
And looking up I saw his face
Outlined against the white of heaven.
I could not see his features well
But felt a wrench of recognition,
A warmth – I had the sudden thought
My father had returned from death;
His murmurings were indistinct
But wormed themselves inside me.
And as he whispered, something shifted,
My mind caved in to peacefulness
My body grunted, twitched –
Untangling from its knottedness
As if the muscles had melted;
The burden of my bones lifted

Sinews dissolved their stiffness
My soul was being cleansed –
Blood returning to my feet,
Fizzing in toes, heels and shins,
Then on my knees I felt more blood
And rising from the steady ground
I raised the world up in my palms
And held it to the sky:
The ecstasy of balancing!
And then that bead of light within,
A concentrated ball of light
Expanded from my neck and shot
Along my floating outstretched arms
Pulsating like two shining wings.

CHROSES

3

I was told I should speak to Melchas, a Median exile in Jerusalem, who had been a priest and was known to speak a lot of 'seeing God'. When I discovered him I found that he was old and becoming senile and, to be quite frank, I couldn't get much sense from him. He talked about the 'light' in a mystical sort of way, but did not seem to know the name of Jesus. When I told him about Jesus and his life and teachings, he insisted I should speak to Chroses, a former friend of his who lived in Ctesiphon, the great city of the Persians. This Chroses was an astrologer-priest and, if he were still alive, had a story to tell, he assured me. I was dubious. But as it happened, one time I had to go to Ctesiphon on business, so I decided to seek him out.

Chroses was a bright, cheery soul, with hair as white as the moon, and he was practically immobile. At first he wasn't sure what I wanted, because he had never heard of Jesus either. But when he heard me speak of Melchas, his eyes softened and he interrogated me about him. Then he told me this story, which I record faithfully, although I have to say I am doubtful of its relevance.

Chroses

If I forgot a constellation's name
I felt I had betrayed a friend.
Each night I'd leave my crippled leg
And rise to join the weightless darkness,
To float among the seeds of stars
Exhaling a godly brilliance
And I would drift without a sound

Through depths of fields of light
Not knowing what was up or down
Until each morning brought me back
To earth, to a dulling of the senses,
A reacquaintance with my lameness.

When I grew older, the salt
Of stars began to lose their savour.
Then I would ask Lord Zoroaster
To liberate me from the future
Unscrolled each night across the heavens
In cold unbending glyphs,
Determining our fate.
I came to hate the certainty
Of that relentless cosmic law.

Then one time I received a dream
Of such intensity it changed my life.
A dream about a pilgrimage.
I told it to my closest friends,
Melchas, Cyrus and Balthus,
Devoted if eccentric priests
Who swore it was prophetic
And claimed it was a call for action.
To my complete astonishment
And contrary to all my pleas and scorn
They were inspired or mad enough
To make a journey to the west
To find out if the dream was true.
But dreams are rarely literal.

It's how they act on you that matters
Not how you act on them.
I never saw my friends again.

My dream or vision was a quest
For some great precious thing.
I had to leave my home
And track the setting sun for days
Across a desert, foothills, mountains
Where clouds were perched as silky turbans
Veiling the purity of turquoise;
And then I walked beside a river
With peeling trees on either side.
At night it was the Milky Way
Leading me through the wilderness
Where scattered boulders glimmered
In strange new stellar patterns.

Then suddenly I found myself
In a familiar place. I knew
It was a village near Jerusalem.
Twilight. A track, stone wall, fields
With clumps of snowy sheep.
I felt I was returning home
And wished the dream would stop
But still it moved. I felt the urge
To look up at the sky, and there
Between the Fishes and the Bull
A surge of light streaked down –
Below it on the ground, a shack.

Its window with a face of gold.

Inside, a lamp was flickering;
Musk of bodies, dung and straw.
A warm contented silence.
I saw four Zoroastrian priests
Prostrate upon the mucky floor,
Their robes as violet-white as snow.
I saw a woman in the corner
Radiating gentle light;
The more I stared, the more the light
Flowed out from her and filled the room
As if my staring was producing it –
I had the thought that she was Love
Nurturing the cosmic seed of light
For she was suckling a child –
I glimpsed the bobbing wisps of hair
And in its face the deepest eyes
Still shining from their other world.

The muscle of my heart unclenched,
Opening and opening as a mother's
Before new eyes of helpless life.
I cried.
            And then I was outside.
In total darkness, lost, panicky –
I stretched my hand to touch something
I shouted out, and stumbled forward
I prayed for help – I prayed to Love
And pictured those two newborn eyes

Unseen behind the sun, the stars.
Suddenly I felt safe, the darkness
Remained, but now it seemed exciting:
Because I could not see my path
Unfolding to the future, I knew
Each step I took would be alive
With accidents and dangers
With unknown possibilities
Alive with marvels, alive with life.

4

Nicodemus was an old friend. I often used to stay with him when visiting Jerusalem. And it was he who helped me tend Jesus's body at the end. He was a good man, conscientious, a fastidious host. He was devout, but not conventional in his worship – he liked to speculate and explore new ideas. Yet there was always something sad about him, and sighs would leak from him without his knowing it. We always ended up on God and justice, those were our themes; and occasionally our conversations would end in rows. He was as obstinate as me but less inclined to nurture anger – he was a natural peacemaker. He told me more than once about the time he first encountered Jesus on his own. It happened in a friend's house late at night.

Nicodemus

A silence lingered in the street,
Listening intently like a spy.
My voice seemed too distinct and loud.
I thought Jerusalem had cocked
Its sixty-thousand pairs of ears,
But no one could have heard us.

I started, eager to explore
My hopes and fears for Israel,
The need for law and purity.
Then I stopped – I felt I'd been a bore.
The lamps threw wavy silhouettes,
Two giant birds, across the wall.
I could not see him clearly.

His head was bowed; and lamp flames lit
His forehead with a patch of gold.
The silence held me riveted.

At last he spoke, deliberate,
Suppressing tiredness from his speech.
'Doesn't this purity of yours
Suggest we should fence off ourselves
And measure out our moral state
Against the tawdriness of others?
But surely this would separate
Ourselves from love – God's love – as well?'
He paused then added snappily,
'Self-cleansing bit by bit is useless.
It just prolongs the agony.
You must be totally renewed
At once, and only love can do this.'

He paused again. Outside, the wind
Waited, then sucking in its breath
It blew the shadows in the room.
'Look, Nicodemus, flesh gives birth
To flesh, and spirit to the spirit' –
He seemed to listen to the air –
'And only spirit brings you love.'

His eyes were glistening in the dark.
He pressed his temples with his fingers;
The lamp flames seemed to spurt and rise
As if new thoughts were fuelling them.
Then with a clap of hands he spoke again:

'You see, you can't discover love
By being virtuous alone;
The I that seeks out virtue is
The I that seeks out purity
And there shouldn't be an *I* at all!
You cannot grope your way to love
By thought or will or sacred books –
You must abandon every hope
That one more pious deed or prayer
Will tip you over into heaven –
Each effort just inflates your self
And shrinks the space reserved for God.
Be still, and wait.
Then the grace of love may come –
And it's like nothing else on earth:
It is as if your soul expands,
A sail blown out by blasts of wind
But gentler, an efflorescence;
Or it's like the sudden thoughtless shock
When plunging in an icy stream
And mind and body bolt together –
You don't have time to think about
The onslaught of that burning water
Because you *are* that cold and heat.'

He spoke with such intensity
I felt quite fevered, almost ill.
But now he slumped. His eyes shut tight.
I let the pause drift on
Then muttering 'thanks' I moved towards

The door self-consciously and told him
I would think further on his words –
At that he jerked his head at me:
'Don't think. Just let yourself be still.'
I forced a smile and watched the bird
Behind him rise in flight
Then left, rejoined the night.

JOHN

5

One time I heard a ship was leaving Sidon for Ephesus. I knew that
John, Zebedee's son and the brother of James, had gone to live in that
great city. So I decided to pay him a visit and combine it with business. It took ten days to get there, including stops at Cyprus and
Rhodes. In Ephesus I discovered from the local brethren that John
was living by himself beyond the city. I paid a boy to guide me
through the crowded streets. There was restlessness everywhere.
Shopkeepers and craftsmen had the air of conspiracy, distraction.
There was talk of violence.

I was glad when the boy led me out of town towards the east. We
walked through endless groves of olive trees, then finally up a hill. It
was more of a cave than a house. His face had changed. His features
were sharper and browner, his hair more wild and white, like Ezekiel
or Elijah. He was friendly, but with a sort of otherworldly distance.
As we chatted we heard far off in town what sounded like chanting
and shouts, even screams. It seemed to go on and on. John ignored it.
It happened all the time, he said. Eventually the distant din subsided,
and John began to talk in earnest. What I remember best was his
account of when he and James and Peter had gone with Jesus to
climb a mountain near Caesarea Philippi. By the time John had
finished it was dark. We sat in silence and watched the belt of Orion
gain brilliance above a hill.

John

We left in early morning darkness
And climbed the foothills in the glow
Of dawn that spread the path before us.

We rested every hour or so
To pray or drink or eat some bread.
He did not say a word to us
And we were too preoccupied
Treading the stony paths ahead
To ask what we were doing there.

By early evening we had reached
The top, a plateau with three cairns.
Far to the west, a haze of sea,
Grey line of mountains to the east,
And at the bottom of the drop
Boulders had turned to pebbles, trees
To tufts of grass or bits of firewood.
We felt like prophets, birds or angels
Rising among the snow and rocks
Breathing the wind, as sharp as ice,
Majestic as the world around us.

The sun was close to the horizon
And twilight hesitated then
Descended like a sacred presence –
He suddenly withdrew from us
And walked towards the mountain's rim.

And as we watched we saw him change:
His body glowed, like white-hot iron,
And then became a spirit fountain –
Light seemed to rise and flow from him
And float in drifts of flakes of snow
The air got brighter, almost crystalline,

A sparkling canopy or sea spray,
It was as if we were inside
A waterfall without the sound,
As if we were inhaling light
Gulping, like fish, the glittering air
And marvelling, and marvelling,
Enfolded in a timelessness
And almost unsurprised to see
Figures appearing out of nowhere:
An angel either side of him,
The three of them quite motionless
Yet seeming to communicate.

We seemed to stare for hours
Before the light became just air
The coruscating motes diminished
The angels faded and were gone.
Alone again, he came towards us
And Peter started babbling on
While James and I burst into tears
Sobbing and laughing soundlessly
Until we felt him touch our shoulders.
Calmer, and drained, aglow, we saw
The world in shades of grey – the snow
The boulders, stones and sky were dingy.
The darkness that had been delayed
Descended on us suddenly.

It seems like only yesterday –
That helpless, joyful ecstasy.

I never thought we would be worthy
To be his witnesses, to see
Those shining figures side by side
Their arms stretched out like crosses
Their bodies made of light – right then
I lost my fear of death, I knew
That nothing could destroy that light.

6

On another occasion I travelled with some companions from Jerusalem to Jericho. We braved the winding descent of that brigand-haunted road, until the palms and houses greeted us with shade and the prospect of rest. I never felt easy in Jericho, with all its heat and windlessness. But the people were always welcoming. My purpose was to see two men who had met Jesus a week or so before he was executed. Bartimaeus and Zacchaeus. I went to visit Bartimaeus first – I was told he used to be something of a celebrity but was now a recluse. We sat alone together in his dusty house. It was after dusk and he did not bother to light a lamp.

Bartimaeus

I don't know why I'd gone to see
The man at all. To ease the boredom,
To cure another dreary day
Perhaps, or curiosity.
Or was it faith that dragged me there
From my exasperated reason?
I have pondered this for years.
Is faith a blinding moment
That comes through grace despite yourself?
Or is it always lurking there
A comfortable familiar thing,
A form of words you reach for
With growing desperation
When every other hope has failed?

That day my boy had led me out
And there we waited in the street
Behind a shifting human fence,
Our patience grilling in the heat.
Eventually we heard a shout
Half-hearted cheering in the distance
Yet still he did not come. My brain
Dazzled, hot, was nagging me to go;
My boy was pulling at my sleeve.
And then I knew he was upon us –
An outbreak of disjointed clapping
The people standing just in front
Burst into sharp applause
Like pigeons startled into flapping;
Next thing I heard this throaty roar
And in the roaring broke the words

'O son of David, pity me!'

A thundercrack.
The hubbub stopped unevenly
Voices collapsed to silent wonder
Then fumbling feet broke up the hush;
People turned to see who'd shouted
And jostled for a better view –
I felt their whispers fly towards me
And someone tugged, and someone pushed.

We shuffled forwards through the crush
Then stopped.
'Your faith has healed you.'

In every word there was a weight,
A penetrating gentleness
Tears bubbled. Manic blinking.
I thought it strange my tears seemed blurred
And I remember thinking that
If tears were blurred then I could see;
The blurring thinned – brighter, brighter
Until a sudden stab
Of light, I crumpled, clasped my face
And felt the cheering burst around me
An arm placed gently around my waist.

It was some months before I saw
The world in ordinary light,
The wonder failing, details smudged,
My flesh less sensitive to touch
My hearing blunted by my sight.
And as the world began to pall
The faith I never knew I had
Began to disappear as well.
I tried to pincer faith and blow on it
As if it were a glowing coal.
But all I did was watch it cool.
Too late I heard him speak to me
In a dream as crystalline as dew:
'You cannot fabricate your faith
Nor can you make it stay by thought –
You must renew it every day
By opening to its openness.'

I tried to keep that holiness
From drifting from my life. In vain.
I tried not trying to maintain it,
And tried and tried: and then I tired.
The voice that roared to him for mercy
Was born of anger, not of faith –
Yet was it rage that healed my eyes?

And was it lack of faith that made
The darkness claim my eyes again?
My nights are night, my days are night.
Still, darkness has its consolations.
At least you know just where you are;
You asked what gift he gave to me:
He brought new purpose to my life,
To blot the memory of light
To forget the faith I never had.

Zacchaeus

7

The morning after I saw Bartimaeus, I found Zacchaeus on the outskirts of the town, washing the exterior of his house. A short man with a bushy beard and cheerful face, he had been a tax collector. But now, he told me, he was devoted to his music. He played the double pipes at weddings and other celebrations. The money wasn't much, but the sound the pipes made was so pure it seemed to cleanse his soul each time he played them. He was eager to be helpful and told me about the time he'd climbed a tree to get a better view of Jesus as he entered Jericho. Later, Jesus came to visit him at home.

Zacchaeus

He sat where you are sitting now.
Just him and his companions
Although it felt like quite a crowd.
Who has a prophet come to stay!
Who comes to see a tax collector
Except to threaten violence?
I could not shoo the smile away.
At first there was an awkward silence.
Someone sighed, and someone coughed.
He looked much bigger than I thought,
Watching the others casually
As if to weigh the atmosphere.
At last he spoke: 'Zacchaeus. Tax.'
He paused. I felt my face burn red.
'You find your work detestable.
But nothing is forever, is it?

And I collect as well – collect
These talents' – he gestured to his friends.
'Perhaps we might exchange a few
Professional tips?' A nervous laugh
From me, and just a sigh from him.

'You're wondering why I've come,' he said.
'You see, I need enthusiasm
To help sustain me on my journey.
Collecting taxes does not mean
A person cannot give out love.
It does not matter what you do
As much as what you are, and give.
I saw you raised up in that tree
Above the crowds of Jericho –
I watched you grinning through its leaves
As radiant as a ripened fruit
And felt your generosity
Like a patch of sun in winter
Or a swathe of warmth you sometimes enter
When swimming in the sea.
We help our lives through small encounters
With friends and strangers, day to day –
A passing smile or cheerful greeting,
A conversation in the street –
When we receive the chance to open,
The chance to change or else be changed
If only for the briefest moment,
And you have helped me on my way.'

We chatted for another hour
Before he stood up and thanked me for
My hospitality and friendship.
As they filed towards the door
I felt quite shaky, emotional,
And jealous of their freedom
To come and go, and for a second
I had an urge to leave with him
And start another life. Instead
I hugged each one of them
And watched them disappearing down
The alleyway that joined the path
Which joined the street that left the town
And rose towards Jerusalem.

8

The village of Bethany was where it is said Jesus raised his old friend
Lazarus from the dead. Lazarus had two sisters, Martha and Mary,
whom I sought out a year or so after Jesus's death. From Jerusalem it
was a gentle stroll along a donkey track through olive groves to the
village – a pleasant outing for an afternoon. They welcomed me as if
I were a long-lost friend, although I did not know them well at all.
Lazarus had gone away for several days and they were eager for some
company, to hear news of other towns. Martha was strikingly tall,
expressive, and quick to laugh to set you at your ease. Mary was
reflective, shy even. Her eyes seemed to gaze on two different worlds
at once. We gossiped for a bit, then when the conversation flagged I
asked them what they remembered best about him. They both fell
silent and looked at one another.

Mary of Bethany

I was obsessed with him.
The constant gnawing for a hint
And mad interpreting of signs
That I was his favourite
The one he loved before the rest.
And mostly – mostly – I was fine,
Until he chanced to smile at me
Then I would blush a prickly red
And curse the others being there
Sharing him out in silly crumbs
As if he were a loaf of bread.

I counted down the dreary suns
Until each festival came round –
Pilgrims arriving all day long
The waft of jasmine in the air
And nights of chanted psalms and songs.
I longed to see his face poke through
The door and hear my name called out;
I visualised his loose embrace,
Rehearsing every word and gesture.
He was the rhythm of my year.

Until one time he spoke of love.
We were talking on the roof
At twilight, breathing in the coolness,
Watching the streets of Bethany
Sink down beneath the flow of darkness
Watching the stars appear above
In ones and twos then sprinklings,
And wondering about our lives,
What would become of all of us.

From nothing in particular
I asked him whom or what he loved –
And wanted to block up my ears.
He thought about it, then he said –
I can remember every word –
That love is not a tight emotion
Compressed towards a single thing
But open and unbounded.
It cannot single out one person,

For she or he would dominate
And make what should be pure and free
Too limited and limiting,
Bereft of generosity.

We sat in silence for a while.
I felt so sad, but calm, quite calm,
Allowed myself a rueful smile.
He gently put his arm through mine.
'Love,' he said, 'does not make choices.
Don't love your friends or enemies,
Because that would discriminate
Between them; simply let it grow,
As wild and fresh as river reeds,
And let its fragrance rise before you
Like aromatic woodsmoke
Which everyone can smell with pleasure
No matter who it is. Dear Mary
Love does not think before it speaks
Love does not judge before it gives
Love does not look before it comforts
Because love cannot help itself.'

MARTHA

9

Mary stopped abruptly, suddenly emotional. We sat there for a while, remembering his voice and gestures. I broke the silence with a light remark and turned to Martha. With a sigh, apologising to her sister, who, she said, had heard it all before, Martha recalled her final meeting with Jesus.

Martha

The day was fresh and bright, and yet
He seemed exhausted; the festival
Was drawing near and building tension,
Bethany crawled with foreigners,
Pilgrims and riff-raff – dagger-men
No doubt; there was a raucousness,
A flowing out of violence
That washed away his natural light.

He saw each one of us alone,
Unusually, to say goodbye;
I did not guess or ask him why.
So there we sat, each waiting for
The other to begin to speak,
Aware of silence thickening like smoke,
Fed by failing sparks of thought,
That trapped us in self-consciousness.
I'd never seen him look so bleak,
His head cast down towards his lap.
The silence had a secret life –
To say a word seemed like a sin,

The breaking of some sacred pact
That would initiate disaster –
Yet how I longed to talk to him
And put my hand on his shoulder.

The window framed the whitewashed wall
Across the street, a world away.
The sun had made the opened door
A sheet of light with golden specks
Yet still the room felt dank, and grey.
I sat there teeming, paralysed,
I couldn't be myself or break
The spell, or look him in the face –
I imagined that an evil spirit
Was fouling the atmosphere;
The distancing intensified:
I felt him moving to a realm
Of darkness I could not reach
And that he had abandoned me –
Perhaps I had abandoned him?
It was as if a winding cloth
Was slowly being wrapped around
Our hearts, removing us from life;
And then there flashed the memory
A cold and hostile memory
Of a childhood springtime day
When I was at my happiest
The world seemed regular and right
And my gang of friends had in a plot

Run off together all at once
And left me standing on my own
To see if I would cry or not.

Judas

Shortly after the execution, I talked to Judas, who had been ostracised by the brethren. They believed he had colluded with the authorities in Jesus's arrest. Judas was not easy to like. I was told that during arguments and debates between members of the inner circle he would throw himself into the fray and completely miss the point. He was a loner, an idealist. He lacked charm, and was brittle and humourless. On the other hand he was patient and dogged, and efficient. Even so, I often wondered whether it was a strength or weakness on the part of Jesus to let Judas come as close to him as he did.

He was living in a shepherd's hut in stony fields a mile or two beyond Jerusalem when I discovered him. He was a mess and had a look of desperation about him. His beard was matted, his fingers like tentacles, grabbing at the food I'd brought him.

Judas

Before the end began
I found him sitting by himself
Inside a stable where he'd go
To flee the vicious dust and noise
Of Jerusalem. I said hello
And kissed his cheek as usual,
Sat down beside him. He did not move
But kept on staring into space.
I, too, could feel the mood,
The brethren flaring, shouting, rows
Or bickering, and crowds, those crowds!
Flowing like refugees of war

With children, chickens, baskets borne
On heads, and everyone so loud
From nervousness, excitement, fears
Except the gleaming clumps of Romans,
Great eagles in their massive towers
With eyes like tips of spears.

I barely recognised his voice –
So childish and monotonous –
But what he said astonished me
Such a relief to hear at last
Something which came from him not 'God' –
That all his life he'd felt alone
(And how my heart leapt at those words)
Not quite a member of the world,
Always unable to join in
The ordinary conversations
Which made him feel an alien,
An orphan doomed to search the earth
For someone who would recognise him.
Not all the time, and he could feign
For a day's or evening's worth
Of company before, again,
The distancing returned to him
And he'd withdraw to pray
And dream of other people's lives.

And then he gripped me by the arm
Like this and said, 'Don't leave me now,
I need you here beside me, Judas.'

And as I felt his desolation
And recognised it as my own
I knew at last that we were one –
God had granted me this prayer.
I saw his destiny was mine –
Outsiders who would change the world!
I told him all the secret plans;
I blurted out – I didn't care –
The middlemen, moles and spies,
The passwords, signs, the armouries
And names of priests and pharisees.
I talked, tearful for the future,
I talked until my soul was bare.

He didn't hear my words.
He looked blank. I looked blank.
Then thought about my broken oaths
Of silence, and felt like retching.
And all he said was:
'Do not leave me here alone
A wind has blown a space
Inside my soul, and in men's eyes
There is a darkness.
I am invisible to love.
Don't leave me here alone
Or something terrible will happen.'

Don't leave me here alone,
That's what he kept repeating,
Joseph, don't leave me here alone.

JAMES

11

Two years after King Agrippa came to power, I went down to Jerusalem to celebrate the Passover, and there I heard that James, the son of Zebedee and brother of John, was staying in the city. The season brought the memories of ten years before – the crowds, the soldiers, and inflated prices.

James was an honest, brave man but headstrong. He was prone to go berserk but quick to make amends. He could be embarrassingly outspoken, and this had made him enemies. He looked just like his younger brother, except he was much heavier, his features slightly coarser. And he was more engaging and direct, less sensitive. We sat and talked in the shade within the Temple precincts, the safest place in town, he said. By this time he was being trailed by the authorities, who knew a troublemaker when they saw one.

James

The tiny window fed mosquitoes
Into the room. I won't forget
The steady chewing of bread
Intrusive sniffing, gulps of wine,
Each conversation stifled by
The airlessness that it created;
And I remember wondering why
I felt no love for anyone.
He looked as if he hadn't slept
His hair fell down like stringy seaweed
His words were too familiar –
I could have mouthed them as he spoke.

He said we had to stay together
To face the coming dangers.
Right then I wasn't bothered whether
We did or not. I didn't care.
We seemed to be well-meaning strangers
Making the best of it because
We knew we wouldn't meet again.
And then he blessed each one of us
In turn. And no one said a word.

Morose, we left that room late on –
So wonderful to breathe the night –
Followed him through the eastern gate
And stumbled up the gloomy slope
Past outcrops and the arms of trees
That loomed like crosses on Golgotha.
Behind, the Temple was a mountain,
Rising against the starry heaven
And streaked by whispering shadows
From countless torches, passing lamps.
And suddenly I felt at one
With everything, with life itself,
Connected with the past and future –
I felt so proud to be a Jew
To hear the singing from the tents
To be a part of this great feast
With Moses looking down on us
And all the kings and prophets too.

He led the three of us away
To a small clearing in the trees,
I was reminded of the time
When he became a torch of light
Up on that mountain in the north,
With angels on his right and left.
Those were the figures I saw
While drifting into sleep, the earth
So welcoming, and pilgrim songs
Mingling in the scented darkness –
Next thing I hear the blurted grunts
Of someone yelling in a nightmare.
I scramble up and see him crouching,
Talking to Peter, or was it John?
And then the thuds of padding feet
Torches moving through the trees
And shouts as if from stricken animals –
The eyes of Satan everywhere –
I don't know what I'm doing, then
My arms are wrenched behind my back
And someone hits my head – the world
Distorts, cracks into sparks,
Hysteria, and voices crying
So loud they would have raised the dead
As if the trees, now come alive,
Are screaming like the dying.

12

On one occasion I had business in Cyrene, a city to the west quite near the coast. I was tipped off to contact a man named Simon, who had apparently been forced to carry the execution beam along the route to Golgotha. It seems the brethren consoled him after his ordeal. Simon was, perhaps, the last to speak to Jesus alive, and so his witness was important to me. In Cyrene I located his home and found him with his mother, who was singing to him softly.

Simon of Cyrene

I was a stranger from Cyrene
Innocent and anonymous
Imagining how it would be
To die slowly on the cross.
And then my dream became a nightmare:
Two soldiers yanked me from the crowd
Two more were holding up the beam
Another shouting in my ear
'When you hold her, find the balance.
Don't move until the weight is even.'
I felt the thud on my shoulder.
I gripped, shifted underneath,
An urgent prodding from a dagger,
My legs too bent to move at first
Straightened. A jab of pain.
A soldier bawling in my face
Ironic cheering at my stagger –
The rhythmic clapping got me going

And people roared off their relief
And let out wild excited yelps.
I told myself obsessively
'This beam is not for me
This beam is not for me ...'
The mercy of that clapping beat
The noise and motion and the weight
Diminished, then silence, the gift
Of glorious unasked-for peace
For suddenly we were outside
The walls and at that charnel ground –
Horizons struck by jagged light
From rips of thunderclouds
And just a few of us were there –
Soldiers had fended off the crowd.

I wasn't certain who he was,
Except the soldiers called him 'king'.
We briefly looked at one another,
He was my colouring and height –
He could have been an elder brother.
The rawness of his broken skin
Made me wince. I heard him whisper,
'She must not stay, she must not stay.'

And then they grab him from behind.
I hear him scream and see the nails
A shiver shreds my spine
Rush of prickling on my skin
My mind and flesh become disjointed

My mind in someone else's body
Or someone's thoughts within my head.
Then it begins.
                    A soldier points
At me and shouts out to a friend:
'Hold on. It's this one for the cross –
This one's the king, not this poor sod –
And who would know the difference!'
They seize me and I scream to God
And wrench my shoulder joints
Then hear them falling back with shrieks
Of laughter – a joke they have rehearsed
So many times before – I sag
Then crumple to the earth.
The world goes dark, then bright, I'm panting,
A fish discarded on the shore
Half feel my body being dragged
And tended to by gentle hands.

At times I feel the same inside
As that young man I was before.
At night I hear the nails and cry
To God to stop the tearing skin;
Sometimes it seems I am the king
And that they took and crucified
The one who wasn't me
The passing stranger from Cyrene
Oblivious of his coming fate
Just standing with the city's dross
Imagining how it would be

To die upon the cross;
It feels so strange that I escaped
And someone innocent was lost –
A person from Cyrene
Who died instead of me.

MARY

13

I had known Jesus's mother Mary ever since my brother married her sister. We'd meet occasionally at celebrations and funerals. She was softly spoken and thoughtful, retiring, and yet she had a reassuring presence, and listened to your words intently. Soon after Jesus was put to death I went to Nazareth to visit her, to pay my respects and see if I could help in any way. I found her calm, even peaceful, and in the event I said virtually nothing. We sat inside the cool of her home and let the sun burn against its thick walls.

Mary

They begged me not to stay and watch him
Even from a distance.
I felt I could send out my love
Even from a distance.
Those three thin spring trees
That should have been in blossom.
At moments such as these –
And God preserve me from another –
You become a stranger to yourself,
Detached and then hysterical.
I screamed, prayed, wept, watched.
Then someone led me off somewhere.

For hours you forget, then days
Go past; you start remembering
Small isolated incidents
And words you never said
And words you never should have said.

The worst thing was the sense
His personality was dead
His past fragmented
Into a thousand tiny moments,
All crawling like bees
Within the hive of my memory.

The journey helped; the trees and homes
Of Nazareth, the goats, vines, fields
Exuded familiarity.
I was composed … I thought I was
Until inside the house I saw
The little fishing boat,
One of the first things he had carved.
Life seemed dark and hard. So hard.

Until there came that night.
I started from my sleep, a noise
Perhaps or something else; I sat up.
At first I thought it was a dream –
A figure standing near my feet –
I bit my hand to feel the pain
And watched, too scared to scream –
I couldn't see his face at first
But then my eyes adjusted:
It looked like him, but far too young,
About the age of seventeen;
I felt so overwhelmed with love
That every drop of fear drained
From me, all sense of sorrowing

Flowed out like water from a skin;
He lifted up his hands to show
His palms, I saw his wrists,
Their lovely pallid glow,
And yet too dull to be an angel's.
I scrutinised my hands as well
To see the difference, looked up
And saw him smiling, laughing,
And I began to chuckle too –
It all seemed so ridiculous –
Until the tears dripped down my cheeks.
I could not move or think or speak
But simply let my body go
And falling and falling I drifted
Into a warm and friendly darkness.

Next day the world was different.
I felt connected to its veins
And laughed and cried at anything;
I swept the floor and fetched some water,
Then in the afternoon I walked
Away from sleepy Nazareth
To let the ground absorb my grief
To listen to the insects sing
To see uninterrupted distance
To feel the breeze around my face;
I walked across a field of grain,
Some trees were coming into leaf
And some were full of shifting light
Full of the spring and green again.

14

From Nazareth I made my way to Magdala, a dingy sort of town beside the Sea of Galilee. It usually stank of fish but this time the wind had purified its breath. And there I found the Mary who was thought to be the first to see him after his death. These appearances of his were strange; it was not clear to me whether they were dreams or visions or something else. It was said he could be touched, physically; but whenever I heard of these blood-and-flesh affairs, I must confess I allowed myself a surreptitious smile.

There had always been a certain distance between myself and Mary, although we spoke more frequently towards the end. I think she thought I was a person of some influence and that I could have been involved much more with the brethren, and she was probably right. I felt she could have been less obvious, less public, shall we say, in her commitment to the cause. So I was wary when I poked my head inside her door and saw her preparing food. She stared at me, as if she did not recognise me, then with a shout of 'Joseph' she ran over and put to flight my reservations.

Mary of Magdala

The thunderstorms had passed.
The sun burnt brightly in the garden
With its bushes and crumbling wall,
And all was watery, awake,
Shining, as at the first creation –
Songbirds, grass and wild flowers,
A fig tree and a fallen branch
Black and twisted like a snake.

I edged my way inside the tomb
And peered.

Emptiness, dampness, and nothing there.

The rock released no atmosphere
Of death, or of anything
Except a penetrating absence.
My head was numb, my heart a bone.

Bending, emerging from the twilight,
I squeezed my eyes and welcomed back
The dazzle of the morning sky
Then glimpsed the bushes to my right
And gasped: they seemed to be on fire –
I saw the flaming wings of angels,
Their feathers burning soundlessly
But never losing shape or brilliance.
Between the slowly moving wings
The faces were as calm as silk
More of the light of moon than sun.
I heard my name called out:
I turned, all goose pimples, spellbound,
And saw a figure standing there.
I stared and couldn't help but shout,
'God, where have you taken him?'
He said my name again.
And then I recognised his voice
Without a thought to hinder me
I ran to hold him in my arms –
My face approaching his, he said,

'Mary, you cannot touch me now.'
He stopped me dead.
And there I stood distraught; aflame;
Just wanting to be held by him.
He kept on speaking, calm and slow,
Consoling, cooling down my brain.

'Mary,' he said, 'you must release
The conversations that we had
The journeys that we shared
And all the love that flowed between us –
Discover them again
In different places with new people.
Our souls are redolent of love
But always moving on and on
Dispensing light and moving on.'

He paused. I stood there like a tree
Immobile, straight, unbending.
His features seemed sharper, refined
His skin was paler than before.
He smiled at all my scrutiny.
'Mary, my body was a vehicle
Confining me, but now I move
As free as unobstructed thoughts –
No sense of willing or of choice;
It's like a sifting of soft light
From moment to moment yet without
The time for moments to occur.
Nothing can grate or modify

The spirit that I have become
The spirit that is given freely
To everyone abandoning
The life that clings to life.
So tell the others what you've seen
And heard, creating everything
From spirit, not from memory,
So they will witness too
The life emerging from my death.
And they can pass the good news on,
Forgetting what was told to them
But making all things new again.
Go, do not hesitate.
Forget the man you knew before
And I shall always be beside you.'

I turned, ran out through the gate
Kept running, looked behind and saw
The angels' wings rise up in flames
Above the wall, and felt the wind
Fly against my eyes, I did not stop,
The puddles were like shining faces
Lying on the ground, with stones
And grass rejoicing in their light.

CLEOPAS

15

One time when I was visiting Jerusalem I made the journey to Emmaus, a village seven miles away, a decent walk before the sun became too hot. I had been told about a certain Cleopas, who claimed that he and a companion met Jesus, miraculously, on the road leading from Jerusalem just after the crucifixion. Another appearance from the dead! Emmaus was a tiny place, more or less a street of shacks. I found Cleopas in a field, tending goats. He was a big but graceful man. His greying beard had bits of grass in it. He asked me who I was and I explained the connections and he immediately apologised, thinking he should have recognised me. We sat in the shade of a tree. I let him take his time.

Cleopas

The sun was reddening on our left.
We listened to our dreary steps
Watched images of Golgotha
That followed us like village dogs.
A donkey passed the other way –
Its eyes were looking straight and down,
The rider looking straight and blind
To our existence. So we progressed
And kept a slow but steady rhythm
Exchanging minimal remarks
Then let a silence overtake us.

Eventually we heard the footsteps,
A pilgrim, as we thought, like us
Returning from Jerusalem.

He came up level by my side
And yet I never really saw him.
I could not see beyond
My thoughts parading death, loss
And isolation through my mind.

When later at the inn he broke
The bread in that hot boisterous room
It was as if a silence rose
Like incense, and I saw his face
At once, was seized by an enchantment,
The sense that only I could see
A person who I knew was dead –
As if I'd stepped inside a dream awake
To meet a loved one from the past.

He said true vision came from love,
Which is a purifying force
That strips corruption, makes you see
The rose that shines within the rose,
Reveals a person's kindliness
Beneath his cunning, hate and spite.
And then he said – these were his words:
'I almost left you at Emmaus
But then you blurted out to me
"Friend, don't go, it's nearly night –
Why don't you stay and eat with us."
And there was something beautiful
In your direct sincerity,
Something so natural and open:

That was the moment when you saw me –
Although the seeing had not reached
Your eyes – not when I broke the bread,
Which was just an outward sign.
Look, I may bless and break the bread
A thousand times hereafter
In all the inns of Palestine
And all the taverns of the empire
And if you have excluded love
Then you may look for me forever
In family, friends and strangers
In every region of the world
But find just dusty soulless bodies,
In everyone you see and hold.'

SIMON PETER

16

Once when travelling from Damascus to Jerusalem on business I broke my journey for a few days at Capernaum by the Sea of Galilee. To my delight I heard that Simon, nicknamed the 'Rock' (ironically as I assumed) was resident in town. I'd always liked him. He was prone to gaffes and swings of mood, but there was not a drop of malice in his heart.

When I arrived at his home I found him talking animatedly with a friend, a shortish, balding man, a pugnacious type. So intent were they in their discussion – about the law and purity – they did not see me peering in at the doorway. At length I coughed and Peter welcomed me in. His friend quickly made excuses and departed. Peter said the old companions were still meeting regularly to share experiences and pray together. New followers were joining them, and not just Jews. He himself was looking forward to going to Rome shortly to help to spread the word. 'It will be a new beginning for me!' he exclaimed with typical enthusiasm.

Simon Peter

I never felt so frightened, free,
As when we left our lives behind,
And set out on that endless journey
Across the desert of the world –
The growing camaraderie
And demons hissing their retreat
As we progressed, the thrill
Of entering some strung-out village:
Loose dogs and children in the street

The gathering of a crowd –
Like crabs the sick ones crawled towards us
And uttered prayers, dramatic groans;
And evil spirits writhed, shouted
Obscenities, and spat, threw stones,
While shifty-looking types lingered
Conspicuously inconspicuously
By trees, in shade or on the fringes.
So wonderful the way
He made the crippled stand again
And sinners beg to be forgiven
With words, just words.
Can you imagine it?
Transforming people's lives with words?

A week or so before they killed him
He spoke to me in confidence.
Till now I've never told a soul.
It was the road from Jericho –
The palms had petered out, the track
Was twisting through the dried-up valley.
Our group was straggling in the sun
The world a glare of floury dust,
And just a steady crunch, crunch …
I walked beside him at the back
For there was a thorn in my mind
That had been needling me for weeks.
I braved the sanctity of silence
And asked him what we were to do
And how we'd organise ourselves

If something were to happen to him.
It was as if he hadn't heard.

We kept on walking side by side
For half a mile before he spoke
With uninhibited fatigue.
'Simon,' he said, 'will you ever learn?
How would you organise the wind?
How would you organise the ocean?
You have been witnessing the way to live
Each day we've been together;
Your letting go your work and home
Has freed you from the past and future –
By living in the present, your life
Becomes successive timeless moments
Each one forgetful of the one
Before – and you ensure that anger,
Ambition, greed cannot survive
Because there is no medium,
No time and space for them to thrive
No sense of self to nurture them.'

We walked another mile before
He spoke again, with urgency.
And it was strange. He read my mind.
'Peter,' he said, 'don't lead the others.
For leaders need their followers
And followers need followers
And then the world is followers
Disputing truth and inspiration.

And you will spend your precious days
On organising, ordering
What must be done and where to meet
And what to teach and how to praise
And what to eat and how to dress –
While your diverted energy
Cannot sustain the love you have.
So if you gather with the others
Make sure your souls are porous
Absorbing truth then letting go;
And it will take a hold of you and grow
Throughout the journey of your life;
Moving before you in the night
And in the dismal days to come
Like a pillar of pure light.'

JOSEPH

17

The witnesses have told their tales. What should be made of them I leave to judgements better than my own. The only thing left I have to do is tell the final story. For those who have ears to hear, as he would say, let them listen now.

Joseph

The waves were fiery, restless,
A comfort in their endlessness –
Horizons like an empty mind
Light glancing from collapsing angles,
The salty wind and spattering mist
The blossoming of the sails …
How could my darkest mood resist
These elemental energies?

But still my mind consumed itself.
What happens to us after death
And to the disembodied soul?
What happens to the soulless body?
Does it disintegrate to dust
Surviving as a dusty memory?
Anger, pleasure, kindness, lust –
Do they maintain their life in life
Beyond, or will we then be angels,
In substance neither man nor woman
Without the personalities
That we exhibited alive
But simply taking messages

From one dimension to another
Like obsequious ambassadors
In silken gold-embroidered coats?
The thoughts kept rocking side to side
On board the broad Phoenician boat
That took me and my precious cargo,
A heavy trunk that reeked of myrrh,
From Palestine, Jerusalem,
The spiky skyline of Golgotha.

Before the end I must confess
I could not keep myself away
But followed him around the city
To hear his every utterance,
Amazed, half-proud and even scared
Of his passion and intensity,
I'd never heard such rhetoric,
As if his life depended on it –
I felt my life depended on it.
For the first time I nearly grasped
The simple beauty of his vision
Its lure of selfless sympathy
With every living thing. Nearly.

I could not give myself to him
Uproot my old familiar ways;
But I could see his path was true:
That love destroys impediments
To living fully in the present;
But as for everlasting life

On which his teaching seemed to hang –
What can I say? I did not know,
Nor did his followers I guessed.
Perhaps I'd seen too many corpses
And did not have the imagination.
It needed more than faith to make
The leap from death to deathlessness.
It made me think what I could do.

Then suddenly the ending came.
That dark unholy day
With thunderstorms approaching fast;
Such helplessness and sense of loss –
That they had taken from this life
Not just a fragile human being
But all the love of God itself.
I saw the body on the cross –
I'd never been so close to death
In such protracted agony:
Then, there, I vowed to honour him,
That poor collapsed and beaten waif,
And what he had been striving for,
No matter what it took or cost.
It came to me what must be done.
The timing had to be just right.
We took the body from the cross
And laid it on the slushy ground
In blinding wind and blinding rain;
We washed and wrapped it in a cloth
Carried it to a wooden shelter

Embalmed it in a makeshift way
Then laid it in the waiting tomb.

Then two days later easterlies
Were scouring out my brain
On board the freighter speeding past
The giant forms of blackened clouds
The fins of charcoal seas.
Such a relief to sail out west
To leave the darkness of Judea
And let the heart digest its grief.
What happens to the soul or spirit
And to the body after death?
Are we transmuted into angels?
Does anything remain of us?
I thought of my Egyptian friend,
A priest from Alexandria,
And how he thought a dead man's breath
Attempted to rejoin its body
And must be given offerings
Of food and drink to nourish it;
And how the body must lie in
A place the spirit knew and loved
To stop its anguished wandering.

We passed the southern coast of Crete
And stopped a day or so at Malta.
Beyond the Pillars of Hercules
We turned towards the northern star.
I watched the constellations rise

In darker gaps between the clouds
Familiarising those strange skies
And I recalled the trip we shared
In what seemed like another life.
I watched the waves beneath the sun
Riddled with liquid ivory;
I watched the waves beneath the night
Supporting us on every side
And guiding this great ship to land;
Then buried under sheepskin hides
I listened to the creaking wood
The rhythmic answering calls of steersmen
Echoing like distant owls
And lulling me to sleep.

One night, on deck, I saw him in a dream,
As clear and potent as a vision
(And this is how my quest began):
He was walking on the tops of waves,
White-flecked and crinkling in the moon,
And leading tiny silvery fish
In shifting shoals beneath his feet –
I saw their phosphorescence
Beneath the surface of the sea
Shimmering in swathes
Like fields of grain swept by the wind,
And felt their pulsing light; I knew
They were the essence of creation –
The particles of life itself –
Gathering then separating

And swirling into other patterns
That glittered with intelligence,
Like flocks of birds or swarms of bees
Or thoughts appearing in a mind,
Before rejoining into one.
I felt my being was that sea
An ocean teeming, tingling
With every form of living thing;
Or rather I should say there was
A feeling of divinity
Because there was no 'I' to feel
But only simple radiance:
Complete, absorbing and unending.
And then he spoke to me and said:
'The body dies but love lives on
In measure with your life on earth.
Everyone is responsible;
And every act of kindness made
While you are still alive
No matter how half-heartedly
Or small and insignificant
Strengthens the universal ties
That flow between each living thing –
The stones and trees and animals
And every human being –
And link this world with all the stars:
Love makes the cords of light
Increase in luminosity
Until the ceiling of the night
Becomes a dome of radiance,

And this is heaven, this is heaven,
The great ingathering of life
Fulfilled at last through holy love
In which there is no separation,
For what you see is what you are –
And all is God, and God is one.'

At last, arriving at the port
It seemed we'd reached another world.
I went and hired some local men
To do the heavy carrying.
The harbour stank with fly-black seaweed.
Donkeys were waiting patiently
Their panniers heaped with hides.
The sun was halfway up the sky
When we made that final journey
Beside the river, through the woods,
The track unravelling the years,
Birds chirruping in tangled trees
Or flicking through the gaps of light
Between the bud-thick branches.
We broke out into sunlit fields
And laboured, sweating, up the hill;
The land was opening behind
In different shades of brilliant green,
The air was colourful and still.
I found the old familiar spring
And called a halt. We drank the water
From the pool, rested and took stock,
Sitting on cloaks strewn on the ground.

I looked for somewhere right, and saw
A butterfly on a rock
Its wings flat out, absorbing sun.
I heaved away the rock, stood up
And looked around the spread-out land
Marvelling at the woods below,
The yellow flowers near at hand
And a large bird floating peacefully
Its wings a fine serrated shadow
And resting on its element
Free of the moving world below.
I knew that I had found the spot
And that no other place would do.

About the Author

Born of Irish-British parents, James Harpur was educated at Cranleigh School and Trinity College, Cambridge, where he won the Powell Prize for poetry. He has taught English on Crete, worked as a lexicographer and is now a poet and writer. He has won a number of prizes and awards for his poetry, including the UK Poetry Society's National Poetry Prize, an Eric Gregory Award, and bursaries from Cork Arts, the Arts Council of England and the Society of Authors. He has been poet in residence at the Munster Literature Centre, Cork, and at Exeter Cathedral. His poetry collections, *The Dark Age* (2007), *Oracle Bones* (2001), *The Monk's Dream* (1996) and *A Vision of Comets* (1993), and his translation, *Fortune's Prisoner: The Poems of Boethius from the* Consolation of Philosophy, reflect his interest in Christian and sacred themes. His non-fiction work includes *Love Burning in the Soul: The Story of the Christian Mystics, from Saint Paul to Thomas Merton.*

Also by James Harpur

The Dark Age (Anvil Press)

James Harpur's fourth collection includes intimate responses to love, birth and death, and explores faith and vision in searching and unsentimental terms. His powerful poetry gives a new perspective on the travels and travails of early Irish saints and on the Syrian pillar hermit St Symeon Stylites. In these and other poems – about the Book of Kells, a monk and his 'star-timetable', and translations from Boethius – Harpur's lyric gift finds moments of illumination and grace in the ordinary as well as the miraculous.

Oracle Bones (Anvil Press)

An Irish monk watching the Black Death edge towards him; a Delphic priest lamenting the passing of an era; an Assyrian entrail-reader receiving more inspiration than is good for him ... Drawing on legend, myth and sacred traditions, James Harpur explores the universal forces that shape people's destinies and the signs by which their patterns are revealed. These concerns coalesce in 'Dies Irae', a long poem in which a Dark Age Christian tries to reconcile his mission to save souls with his own sickness, physical and spiritual.

'James Harpur is not in the least like anyone else ... His is an amazingly consistent voice, compelling in its intensity. If you're brave enough, read him. He will take you into a world you will find difficult to forget.' R.J. Bailey, *Envoi*

'This is serious stuff ... a map of heaven and hell, of prayer and meditation, of redemption and of unity ... It remains only for the rest of us to catch up, and catch on.' Michael Killingworth, *Magma*

'Harpur takes the stuff of superstition – a Celtic monk, a Delphic priest, an Assyrian extispicist, a superannuated auspex – and gives it a persuasively timeless, often disturbing significance ... *Oracle Bones* offers a kind of religious poetry. It does not, however, carry a whiff of the 'pious' – rather, it has 'a sense of the sacred running in parallel to the quotidian'. Peter Reading, *TLS*

'The movement of the verse is beautifully controlled, the employment of rhyme wonderfully delicate. Harpur's craftmanship articulates a sense of profound spirituality – especially in 'Dies Irae', a long poem, spoken out of the Dark Ages, that I felt compelled to read over and over ... . Anthony Haynes, *The Tablet*

THE IONA COMMUNITY IS:

+ An ecumenical movement of men and women from different walks of life and different traditions in the Christian church
+ Committed to the gospel of Jesus Christ, and to following where that leads, even into the unknown
+ Engaged together, and with people of goodwill across the world, in acting, reflecting and praying for justice, peace and the integrity of creation
+ Convinced that the inclusive community we seek must be embodied in the community we practise

Together with our staff, we are responsible for:

+ Our islands residential centres of Iona Abbey, the MacLeod Centre on Iona, and Camas Adventure Centre on the Ross of Mull

and in Glasgow:

+ The administration of the Community
+ Our work with young people
+ Our publishing house, Wild Goose Publications
+ Our association in the revitalising of worship with the Wild Goose Resource Group

The Iona Community was founded in Glasgow in 1938 by George MacLeod, minister, visionary and prophetic witness for peace, in the context of the poverty and despair of the Depression. Its original task of rebuilding the monastic ruins of Iona Abbey became a sign of hopeful rebuilding of community in Scotland and beyond. Today, we are about 250 Members, mostly in Britain, and 1500 Associate Members, with 1400 Friends worldwide. Together and apart, 'we follow the light we have, and pray for more light'.

For information on the Iona Community contact:
The Iona Community, Fourth Floor, Savoy House, 140 Sauchiehall Street, Glasgow G2 3DH, UK. Phone: 0141 332 6343
e-mail: ionacomm@gla.iona.org.uk; web: www.iona.org.uk

For enquiries about visiting Iona, please contact:
Iona Abbey, Isle of Iona, Argyll PA76 6SN, UK. Phone: 01681 700404
e-mail: ionacomm@iona.org.uk

Wild Goose Publications, the publishing house of the Iona Community established in the Celtic Christian tradition of Saint Columba, produces books, CDs and digital downloads on:

- holistic spirituality
- social justice
- political and peace issues
- healing
- innovative approaches to worship
- song in worship, including the work of the Wild Goose Resource Group
- material for meditation and reflection

For more information, please contact us at:

Wild Goose Publications
Fourth Floor, Savoy House
140 Sauchiehall Street,
Glasgow G2 3DH, UK

Tel. +44 (0)141 332 6292
Fax +44 (0)141 332 1090
e-mail: admin@ionabooks.com

or visit our website at
www.ionabooks.com
for details of all our products and online sales